BELIEVE IT

OR NOT

BELIEVE IT OR NOT

JEAN
MONAHAN

*for Irene
to a fellow poet
thank you so much
for listening today
BPL 4/8/2006
Jean Monahan*

ORCHISES WASHINGTON

Library of Congress Cataloging-in-Publication Data

Monahan, Jean
Believe it or Not / Jean Monahan.
p. cm.
ISBN 0-9 14061-77-1 (alk. paper)
1. Title
PS3563.05159B45   1999
811'.54-dc 21 98-17119
                    CIP

Some of the poems in *Believe It or Not* first appeared in the following maga-
zines: *Chelsea*: "With the Flesh Remaining," "One Hundred Days of a Hermit
Crab"; *Columbia: A Magazine of Poetry and Prose:* "The Concert"; *compost*:
"Every Knot Was Once Straight Rope"; *Graham House Review*: "Gretel, Lost";
Nimrod: International Journal: "Lessons of the Eyeteeth," "The Gift"; *Poetry Inter-
national:* "Lonely In Eden," "Wind in November"; *Salamander:* "Canadian
Geese in Exaltation"; *Seneca Review*: "Medusa Cuts Her Hair"; *Snake Nation*:
"When You Love Somebody"; *Zone 3*: "You Can Lead a Horse to Water." "In
the Cafe Angst," "The Laughing Cow," "Gretel, Lost," "Chain Poem" and
"Canadian Geese in Exaltation" were chosen by Vijay Seshadri to win the
1992 Open Voice Award, sponsored by The Writer's Voice, West Side Y, NYC.
These same poems, along with "If Wishes Were Horses," "Misery Loves Com-
pany," "When You Love Somebody" and "One Hundred Days of a Hermit
Crab," were awarded the first annual (1993) Bruce Rossley New Voice award
from *96 Inc.*

Orchises Press
P.O. Box 20602
Alexandria, VA
22320-1602

G 6 E 4 C 2

With special thanks to the Yaddo Corporation for time spent in good company, beauty and solitude during the summer of 1994. Special thanks to D. Nurkse, Martha Rhodes, Sabra Loomis, Stephanie Strickland, Louisa Solano, Chris Millis and Betsy Lerner for their encouragement and support. Gratitude for the wisdom of Ruth Drasin and Paula Gillis-Ojemann, and for the fortification of family and friends, including Debi Libuda, Nona Mahoney, Steve Sullivan, Jack O'Connor, Madeleine Stein, Janice Vaughn and Melissa Zieve.

Book design by Debi Libuda

FOR JOE FLORES

TASKMASTER
AND MUSE

Contents

Believe It or Not

The Gift

Gretel, Lost

The Laughing Cow

Lessons of the Eye Teeth

My business is to record all that people say, but I am no means bound to believe it.

HERODOTUS, VII. 152

BELIEVE IT OR NOT

S T U C K

According to a 1993 press release from the Butterball company, a woman called the emergency hotline on Thanksgiving day to report that her pet chihuahua had jumped into the cavity of the family's turkey and was stuck.

–News of the Weird, 1995

He is of the desert, a tumbleweed tuft,
scrap from some great cactus combing its hair in the wind.
His too-bright eyes recall the fervor of pilgrims

crossing parched earth; his acute lament
like the shriek of cicadas on their one afternoon of sex.
Who dares point the finger? The wisest

among us has fled the safety
of hard ground. After we are swallowed whole,
we ask: *how shall I hide my nakedness, how shall*

I surface? When we look up, all we see
is the temple of the ribs, that holy cave. This is the tender trap,
the place where the heart lived. Here we can swim,

really swim, in the idea of love.
The heat of happiness lingers in every cavity.
The sound of it: *thump thump, thump thump*: keeps

time with the breaking waves,
with the schools of fish like schools of hearts,
drifting through the sea, drifting through the nets.

Now comes the huge hand of destiny,
squirming through the opening like a giant squid.
This is it. Just when we think we're stuck, we're caught.

LONELY IN EDEN

Single male, age unknown,
lives alone in Paradise.
God knows why
jack-fruit and jasmine,
waterfall and moon-
light won't suffice.
Woe am I, who shapes
earth into my own image, loves
only myself. Other, wherever you are,
send a sign: color in the sky,
dream in my sleep. Must
be of the same heart, bare
of face and limbs. Must
be able to speak, make fire, sin.

THE SECOND WIND

Is soft, deliberate.
Has nothing to do with sky or air.

Part iron and nickel, part fire.
The magnetic blood of the earth. The power core.

It enters the room through the wick of a candle,
budding into flame beneath your hand.

It enters the body through the lines in the palm:
head, heart, life.

You can feel it; it has weight. A catalyst, it can uproot.

The second wind cannot push.
It must be caught.

Prodigal, it pulls at you from the four corners of the earth.

Home is everywhere the needle points.

QUITTING COFFEE

Bruised, hoarse, I crawl out
of the woods after years of feeding on roots
and the long bones of wild animals.

Already, my ability to see at night
is fading. The soles of my feet
soften like soaked burlap.

I lived in a tree, I slept in snow.
Down on all fours, I could leap
straight up and take a deer.

Now, eating with a spoon,
I watch the mouths of those
who feed me. I can no longer feel

the moon, stroking my back
with bony fingers, the jittery
whisk of fire through cattails.

The mouths make such sounds
as wind in winter. I listen hard, harder.
So I return to the fold: wild-eyed, still craving.

LUCKY

"Lucky, a German Shepherd guide dog, led his first owner in front of a bus, and the second off the end of a pier. He pushed his third owner off a railway platform just as the Cologne to Frankfurt express was approaching, and he walked his fourth owner into heavy traffic, before abandoning him and running away to safety. Asked if Lucky's fifth owner would be told about his previous record, his trainer Ernst Gerber replied: "No. It would make the owner nervous, and that would make Lucky nervous. And when Lucky gets nervous, he's liable to do something silly."

—Europa Times, 1993

In Luck, we are all reckless, shameless, helpless;
We go on Instinct, even if it is not our own.

When Luck is my shepherd, I do not want.
I am kept, I am told which way to turn.

Led beside water, I taste the sea on my tongue.
Crossing the avenue of Hope, the demons howl and bark.

I pour myself out like wine; my heart melts like wax.
Yea, though I walk through the valley of Dark,

I stand fast at the screeching track and fear no harm.
Luck is the panting heart, the tug on the arm,

the nose, the bite, the chain. When Luck commands,
I obey. I trust to Luck, that my Luck will change.

FORTUNE

Speak only well of others,
let none guess your least weakness.
Soon you'll be the honored guest
at innumerable parties and gatherings.

You were born for greatness;
few of your friendships will be lasting.
The price of success: suspicion,
self-doubt and misunderstandings.

Silence is weighty, peace fragile.
The next person you meet holds the key
to your survival. Despite our best intentions,
everything happens. There's portent

in a stranger's glance, poetry in the overheard
words of others. Even before your fortune
breaks, the answer you've been waiting for
has scrawled itself across a twist of paper.

HALVED HEAD IN
FORMALDEHYDE

He thinks he has seen it all.

Where once he was ordinary, ignored,
now the world files past him,
open-mouthed.

Outside the window:
the whistle of a train,
the return of spring,
the body's slow slide toward death.

Nothing will change him now;
he is eternal in his acid heaven.

Sallow Santa suspended in mirth,
he seems to wink at all who pass,
the skin on his cheek and brow
the color of aged cork.

He has no need to remember
the look on her face, the slam of a door,
the squeal that shook the birds from the trees
and the warm wind that would not cease.

Down the hall, other cabinets showcase
Siamese twins joined at the mouth,
a torso unzipped like a suitcase
to show its neatly-packed contents.

These are his heroes, and his friends:

the man who goes on spilling his guts
well past his mid-life crisis, not the least
bit unnerved by his own vulnerability;

the sisters who learned in the womb
the pure joy of a like mind;
the difficulty of finding that elsewhere;

and so they emerged, stillborn, mid–

sentence, and then went on telling
each other their dreams.

Mystery, misery: nothing much lasts.

Change exists outside his box,
something warped and warping
that can no longer touch his heart or mind.

For once in his life he knows who he is:
the same man he was yesterday
and will be tomorrow.

The thought of this keeps his eye bright.

WHAT WE TALK ABOUT
WHEN WE TALK ABOUT LOVE

The flight of thought across an open face.

A Dutch door, a threshold, a latched gate.

In the back meadow, the hay bows
before the arc of the scythe,

the tallest trees brought down
by the invisible twine of the grape.

A bee that circles a container of honey,
how the strangest hive can still be a home.

The sea of dream we all row, alone.

A well so deep we can't see ourselves in it.

The bucket we lower into darkness.

The water that slakes our thirst.

Eating a Peach After Kissing You

With my whole body I taste these peaches...
> —Wallace Stevens, "A Dish of Peaches in Russia"

My eye can't accept such intact enticement, my tongue such sensuality.
I hold in my palm a tiny planet the color of sunset, and want to cry.
Instead, I bite the rude cleft near the top, where the fruit clung
To the branch. There is that fuzz on the cheek, the unexpected blush,
I must lick before I rip and chew. What ecstasy to have a mouth full
Of juice, a pulp so shivering against the tooth I dare not swallow.
What else is lovemaking, if not dilemma? In each kiss, I know the shock
Of the first nip, when a whole world of sweet lay waiting to be consumed.
I forget the middle of the peach, where the dark wood of your shut
heart loomed.

Believe It or Not

For fifty years, the man ate eggs.
Not one a day, sunny-side-up, or ten,
but eighty each morning, raw.

This takes a discipline few have.

Elsewhere, an Irishman yodeled for ten hours straight,
a New Yorker with 31 million in the bank
owned one dress and ate her porridge cold.

He was 7 feet, she was 8.
They wed in the shade of a large oak.
Across the world, a man wrote

letter after letter, envelope after envelope,
until two letters shy of four thousand
his pen ran dry.

How does anyone have the courage to lie down at night?

While we sleep, somebody dreams
the world's longest recorded dream;
while we snore or lie awake,

lips meet
underwater in breathless kisses,
a man cracks jokes

to himself, hour after
hour, plates spin
on the ends of sticks,

thread passed
through the eye of a needle
thirteen thousand times.

No part of the world is not in the contest.

A bee hummingbird is smaller than the eye of an ostrich.

Deep in the Niger desert,
thirty miles from the nearest
tree, a recluse baobab

lived by its wits
until the day a jeep
accidentally backed into it.

Nothing, not even posterity,
will protect you from
your singular destiny.

The man struck by lightning seven times
in the end died
by his own hand.

THE GIFT

THE GIFT

Sleeping Beauty, revised

I am the thorn in everybody's side,
the feared guest. They see me
as a gift they can send back.
They have twelve gold plates and one
gold girl; I am her thirteenth
godmother, uninvited to the feast.

There's a silence in the hall
when I stride in, snow in my shawl
and lashes. There's a pin-prick
in my heart until I see her, reaching
for me and laughing. Innocence
knows what comes to bless it.

Years from now, in all the tales
told, I will be the vengeful crone,
the evil fairy. They will say I struck
you from the thick weave of family
before you could bloom. In fact, your
life will be rounded with a long sleep,

a valley of charm you'll drift across.
There will be mountains beyond
and work, the sharp work of the soul,
when you finally awake and learn
what being alive means. In time,
you'll see every other gift:

intelligence—beauty—virtue—wit:
tarnish with age and compromise.
There'll be the months when you look
into the cracked mirror of doubt and
remember the days of merrymaking
in your father's hall, that fortress of

thorns. Remember then, Briar Rose,
what I bequeath now: in place of the
ordinary spinning—suitable suitor,
suitable life—I give you a difficult
blessing, a master for whom you'll toil
to the last drop of blood through your heart:

I give you the curse of enchantment,
I give you dreams, I give you art.

L O R E L E I L O U N G E

Nothing prepares you for Lorelei Lounge.

At the top of the stairs, a blinking L of neon,
a babble of conversations
you won't be invited to join.

Everyone pays at the door,
each according to need.
No grease for the palm,
they want you to sign in blood.

Now your table is waiting, it is even impatient.
It has a glass eye full of ash
and a deep scratch.

If the waiters look familiar,
it's because they bear a family resemblance
to whomever they serve.
Order whatever you like,
they only bring one drink:
water, on the rocks,
with a twist.

At a certain hour, salt air
curls into the room and the curtain lifts.

Six women, no two dressed alike,
stare back at the audience,
their eyes huge and dark.

They are exactly as everyone imagined
they'd be: long-haired, bereft and inviting.
Every chair is a tiny prison; no one can leave.

When finally the Lorelei sing,
the silence is deafening.

RHAPSODY IN BROWN

"Gordon Davey, 30, was named Britain's most boring man after he waxed rhapsodic about his extensive collection of brown paper, which he said has fascinated him ever since he was an art student. Said Davey, 'I shall obviously have to try to be more interesting and less obsessive.'"

–Reuters, 1994

He remembers the garden, the bark
on the Tree, gold-and-olive flecks
in the scales of the rippling snake.
After the bronze flash of godly insight,
he sees copper-colored fingers, his own,
pressing seeds into earth. Her chocolate breasts.
The buff crown of the child thrust
into light.

There were days, weeks, at sea,
maroon waves. The stench of the ark.
The dark calm of the beasts.

He remembers the jagged knife
that sundered the great body
of the world: torso drifting north,
south. Fire, lava, ice.

Roaming each part: desert–plain–mountain–swamp:
he sees everywhere sand, dust, rock and mud.

Soon, there is hair and skin in every shade of brown.
Brown is the vocabulary of all he loves.

One afternoon, sitting in sun,
he pokes a twig into a basin of pulp.
He is about to invent parchment, recorded
history, a common ground for thought.

Each scroll will be a piece of modern art,
already splendid when the first ink
dots its surface with meaning.

Each sheet a different shade of brown.

WORK TAKES A HOLIDAY

Seaside towns captivate most.
Think of the possibilities:
miles of untidy coast,

busloads of debris
to comb through, dispose.
Best of all, the sea

makes it sport: no sooner
the shell pocketed, the weed
raked into bonfire

piles, then new iridescent
fragments are flung
ashore. Though she's tried

holidaying elsewhere,
the results were usually disastrous:
surveying a live volcano,

she ran amok calculating lava flow
and how it might be harnessed;
touched down in a tropical forest

and nearly went to pieces
at the blizzard of prismatic feathers
dropped by shrieking, insouciant

parrots. In the early moments of daybreak,
Work recalls the way moss shawls
trees in the Olympic rain forest,

how untold stalagmites
are stacking up like loose change
in Earth's deepest pockets.

It is something of a curse,
Work's been told, her demand
for system, cleanliness, rules.

Late at night, what hurts most
is the knowledge there is a disorder
she hasn't even dreamed of,

derangements so fundamental
no amount of time—off
could straighten it all out.

She has set her legions—bees,
ants, worms—in perpetual motion,
and still the world defies subordination,

ignores the laws of force, falls apart,
reforms. At yet another seaside resort,
on the seventh day of her latest break,

Work stops a moment to rest. Above,
the cosmos turns, right on cue.
It's never missed a beat since the day

she made it: the constellations sweep
the clouds away, the Milky Way
flushes the whole with dew. She lies there,

thinking: at least *this* has never failed
me, and finds the strength to smile, rise.
Behind her, unnoticed, a star falls.

CHAIN POEM

Please don't ignore this poem.
It has circled
the world nine times,
leaving behind
a swath of good fortune
bright as the Milky Way.
Written by a young seamstress
in Lima, Peru,
the original is now held in Lansing, Mich.
Even if you are not superstitious
send 20 copies out quick;
in 4 days magic
will be yours. Now, you might not believe
in fairies, how they pollinate
the air with their fairy dust,
but, even as your eyes seize upon this page
little charms fly up then swirl back,
brief as snowflakes in a paperweight.
This is not a joke. Be sure the poem
leaves your hands within 96 hours.
Send a copy to anyone you care
about; send your copies wide and far.
Then sit back and wait.
Tango with the dog. Plant a flower.
Kiss someone you love on the lobe
of each ear. Four days later, good
luck in some form—good news, lottery stub,
reciprocated love or answered prayer—
will arrive, by mail, at your door.

P.S. Send no money. The good luck's here,
  in the words.

MEDUSA CUTS HER HAIR

Something in the curl wants out.

✳

You think you know something about love,
have a clear idea of your own value.
Then your friends stop speaking
when you enter a room, turn a cold eye
on your antics, your pleas, your parting curse.

✳

Lately, I've let myself go.
Strange thoughts spring from my scalp.
They have a life of their own.

I think about striking out, striking back.
I think about curling into a knot,
and never encircling another again.

✳

What is it I keep hearing,
in waking and in sleep?
Little voices, secrets, fears.
Every wish I ever had, every hurtful
word I've said. They do not leave,
but hiss in the head, weaving
together until they sprout anew.
There are lies caught in my locks;
memories of happiness, too.

＊

He said he was a hairdresser,
would trim my tresses
by looking into a mirror.
I agreed to keep my eyes lowered.

Think of it: the snip of scissors,
a strange man's fingers,
oil of aloe, henna, citrus.
Nervous, his limbs jiggled;
I fell in love with his legs
as he circled my chair.

＊

Where is the man who cut my hair?

People tease me, say I've lost my head.

Now, the world softens under my stare.

E v e n i n g   i n   t h e   V i l l a g e
o f   A l s o   G o d

outside Budapest

Across train tracks,
on a white backdrop,
a sign for your town:
Also God. A dog runs up

and begs a scratch;
cherry trees in bloom
loose a fluttering,
fruit perfume.

You tell
how deer sometimes steal
to your back fence; how bees
buzz with such zeal

you can't sleep; how
every birthday you roast a pig,
invite the whole village,
twigs from the trees

sacrificed to the fire
when, late at night,
it threatens to go out.
Then and there,

I know the shaky feel
of spring when buds open
under a full moon
and bees navigate by unnatural light.

Host, I hope you will forgive
if tonight I dream
I am the white-hot pit,
the slaughtered pig.

THE CONCERT

Isabella Stewart Gardener Museum, Boston, March 18, 1990

Later, even the courtyard cyclamen
appeared unnaturally bright with omen,
but the truth is, I went to the museum
feeling sad and bored, but nothing more:
upstairs, I imagined falling asleep

on the dark and echoing Moravian tiles.
In the last hour, I stood before Vermeer's
The Concert—a 17th century music room
where three figures had gathered, impromptu.
The pale yellow sleeve of the one who

played was like a caress that falls just short
of abandon, restrained, as it was, by the
rectangle of orange on the back of the man's
chair, and the pale green dress of the woman
singing. I felt I was seeing for the first time:

I stood, ruled by the light, until everything
beyond the frame faded, straining to hit the
right key before the man I had fallen in love
with, the man who sat, staring into the scene
painted on the harpsichord's lid, whose rapture

mocked my own, completely. When the guard
announced the hour of closing, a voice
in my head urged: *look again at the painting!*
I returned, briefly, before leaving. That
night, *The Concert* was stolen. Never again

will the tile in that room bear the weight
of us all in one unbroken plane of existence.
I have since learned how the unattainable
draws the strongest of us in, how lost
worlds, painted or imagined, close

the listener in a haze of silence. I have
come to believe that the one who wore
desire on her yellow sleeve reached
up and closed the harpsichord lid
when at last the concert ended.

GIFTS I'D GIVE YOU

The moon skimmed from the pond
and held in the hand. How it oozes,
beginning to ferment.

A full tank of gas and no plan.
Passages memorized for the long tunnels.

The dress I would wear after
we made love. The room where we would first
break fast.

The key to the house, the teapot, the salt
unshaken by the things that have come to pass.

A secret shame, deep belief,
imperfect love. Constancy, effort, a vow.

My breath away at the sight of you.
The words right out of my mouth.

MEMENTO MORI

When you look upon the wing
of a sleeping bird, the eye that keeps time
with the moving light; when you whelm
the tunnels of the nose with the cinnamon
of breath; after you've memorized a lake at night,
the clarinet sex of the loons, the way wind
tongues the bowls of the dunes, making a sound
like waves: air on quartz; remember then and always
that the life that lives in the body never rests,
monotonously productive as a hive of wasps,
that the inspiration for art is the blood tides
through the heart, the splendid, conjoined rhythm
of sinews and veins and bones. In the illuminated
panels of the Florentine school, the holy
have never forgotten how they had to pass
from one poor life to the perfect next;
at the hour of their death, a corona
appeared to balance lightly on the crest
of the scapula, although we are never shown
the actual apparatus of the halo. In some
of the images, the sky is no larger than the eye
of God, the wise stumble, martyrs
retain the instrument of their torture—
grill, rope, hatchet, fire. This one seems
to be saying: *remember that you have to die*
means remember that you have to live.
He holds out his memento like a gift.

GRETEL, LOST

WIND IN NOVEMBER

I begin as a secret someone lets slip,
a story with no ending, a bad dream.

Where is home ? I think as I lift
my one wing, Air, and my other, Fire.

When I reach the river, I trouble the water.
As I cross the plain, I scatter the elk.
Hurry ! I mouth to the hawks
on the mountain. *The sky is a cage:*
I must escape.

Am I something you said? *Yes.*
Am I something you dreamt? *Yes.*

The world is an egg.
I clutch it in my claw
and rock and rock the sleeper awake.

The night is full of ears, the story is at hand.
Listen: I'll tell you how it ends.

IN THE CAFE ANGST

If you order a cup of coffee in the Cafe Angst
don't despair

when the waiter brings it over
wearing the slightest sneer

on his middle-brow face;
he'll neatly palm

the cake crumbs
of the one who ate before,

then shower
the ring of birds

beneath the tree at the edge
of the garden.

If you prefer your Angst
enlightened, as well as sweet,

he'll gladly tong a pair
of cubes, pour

a stream of cream
into the eye of the inky hurricane.

The moment he moves off,
emotions, like milky clots,

swirl up
from the depths.

Here comes the fear
of losing your place,

which billows on the heels
of losing a loved face;

next comes the grief of sipping alone,
and grief for the joy of leaving home;

now a howl of real hunger: *will
you ever have your fill ?*

and a voice that asks
was there something else

*you wanted
or shall I bring the bill?*

Herr Waiter stands waiting, barely patient.
About now you notice the dim resemblance:

before you stands
the middle-aged Hansel,

who once strewed
the all-important path

home with bird food,
then feigned despair

when the birds ate their fill.
If there's nothing more ...

he palms your coin, then turns to go.
Back in Angst's kitchen—about the same time

you reach the corner,
where the body of the little martyr

of the intersection lights up
danger-red—Herr Hansel brings

the thick china lip
of your cup to his lips,

and slowly, and with the sweetest
addiction, drains the dregs.

CANADIAN GEESE IN EXALTATION

I know now
I could not grow
older without them.

Headed south,
they drag
the doubly-woven cloth

of autumn
across the sky-cage,
opening us up

to whiteness,
and chill.
And each time

their tremendous
honk—which is a cross
between

a bullfrog's grunt
and the bray of a rusty gate—
pulls me up

to where I remember how
to hear what they've said:
turn now, lift, straight

until you see me drop;
they like to aim right
for the heart

of the sky
and go at it, unswerving.
If I

could obey the call to fly
I'd know what
exaltation is! It's not

for lack of direction
I find myself still
bound to earth:

this time every year
the sky grows dark
with streams of arrows.

Listen: I have chewed
my own wings
so often

my words thicken
with wax. *Hush!*
Behind night clouds

another V of geese goes
where it knows
it must.

SLEEPING IN EARTH

To love is to be led away/into a forest where the secret grave/is dug.

—David Ignatow, "Rescue The Dead"

Except for the absence of dreams,
I remember sleeping well,
the welcome dark, your voice,
the mild and nostalgic musk
which lay lightly on your arms
and chest. I remember love's
lassitude on your breath, the languor
in your crying out, marks left
where we sank into flesh.
I lost my sense of smell
first, then earth blocked my sight,
filled my ears, stopped my mouth.

Unearthed, I lie like one dead,
blinking into the sun. Hunger returns,
then thirst, followed by ghastly music
as the ear's inner bell relearns to ring.
I can't tell how long I've slept, but for
my pale fingers, the musty smell
as my nose wakes up to the world.
When I dream again, the woods are full
of figures in woolen coats, hurrying home
through the bent rays of dusk. Touching
my teeth, my tongue tastes blood
and my old voice hardens to a howl.

THE CASE OF THE
WILD CHILD

Among the cases of wild children discovered over the last seven centuries, more than
fifty have been documented. The list includes the Hesse wolf-child; the Irish sheep-
child; Kaspar Hauser; the first Lithuanian bear-child; Peter of Hanover; the second
Lithuanian bear-child; the third; the Karpfen bear-girl; Tomko of Zips; the Salzburg
sow-girl; Clemens, the Overdyke pig-child; Dina Sanichar of Sekandra; the Indian
panther-child; the Justedal snow-hen; the Maurentanian gazelle-child; the Teheran
ape-child; Lucas, the South African baboon-child; and Edith of Ohio.

–Russ Rymer, *Genie*

Praise for my pink madonna.
The spouts on her milk-mountain
taste like cotton. She is an abalone
shell turned inside-out, a bristly
blanket. Her lullaby tells
of the treasures to be found in dirt.
Late at night, she steams like lava.
I only fear her nose, swift and cunning
as a hand.

✳

Dear head, thrust like the barrel
of a gun up close to smell my breath,
what big teeth you have, what deep
eyes, fond and fierce. I think the moon
has fallen into them, they are so yellow
and full. The rough tongue is nonetheless
sweet. It tastes of the blood of life.

*

My mother is as big as a hill,
steadfast as a pine. She would climb
the sky to satisfy. Every spring
she rises from hell to spread flowers.
All winter she sleeps—her paws,
furry axes, my cradle.

*

My mother is a spotted shadow,
an upright meadow. Nimble,
she teaches me to leap like wind.
Humble, she teaches me to nod,
nuzzle. Now we go

up the slope to where
flowers poke from the snow.
She teaches me to herd, flee.
If she could, she would carry
me.

*

Mother, you are as small
as my heart. I hurt to see
you peck at nothing. Why
don't you flee this barren
kitchen? Left behind,
I'd weave a cloak
from your fallen feathers,
expand your abandoned nest.
I know where to find
the seed, the berries.
I know why and when
to sing.

*

My mother is a thief.
She comes upon the helpless
with her teeth, remorselessly
carries morsels home. She is a piece
of night streaking through the day,
an arrow from the underside.
My mother will not swerve,
only survive. I learn from her sleek.
The skin on my knees and hands
has grown paw-hard.

*

Now I lay me down to champ.
The grass is a sliver of silence.
The hills are a kingdom of peace.

Now I lay me down to dream.
The boulders keep me safe.
Her body my scrap of fleece.

Now I stand up to bleat.
She has lambed a tiny white heap.
Rain begins, now wind, now grief.

GRETEL, LOST

What can we be to each other now? Before
we found the house, how brief your smile was,
but how true, how rough the collar
of the great coat we buttoned ourselves
into night after night, like twin worms
in a cocoon. The unfamiliar trail,
when you held my hand, was full of charms.
I see you at the stream, mouth like a pail:
brimming; me impatient for berries
you insist on tasting first, to see if they're
poisonous. What if there had been no house, no scary
hoots from the woods, no carrying ourselves over
that threshold with the promise of food,
a real bed? Hansel, it was good, I could see
myself growing fat with you, chopping wood,
waking up good in the gingerbread house. She
who tried to kill, she of the glazed glass and tart
apples candied to the windowsill, never meant
you harm. Her taste for life, for raw heart
on her daily plate, was just not
the way you wanted to live. By now I'll bet you see
your white cat gleaming on the roof, a wee ·
shaving of smoke curling out of the chimney,
are found again, home. Since you have found me
out, have seen my temper blaze, my treachery, my fire
for things not of your world, you should know that I am lost
again, in other words, myself again, the boss
of my own impossible house, who loved you
            even as I built the pyre.

WHAT THE EYES IN THE BACK OF THE HEAD SEE

The full moon in the sky
when half its face is draped in black.
The reel that casts the clouds,
the rope a spider hangs by.
Centipedes and silverfish, a broken diamond
necklace threading the spikes
of a wrought-iron gate. The grace
in a sow's gait and slow close
of rose petals when darkness
falls. What's seen when a mirror's
mica peels. The careful conceit
lovers daily eat to renew their hunger;
the glee behind anger. There are mountains rising
in a handful of sand, catacombs
beneath living coral. Anything that stretches
toward infinity, the eyes in the back of the head see
its eventual returning: the longing
in the one leaving, the end,
the beginning.

THE LAUGHING COW

THE LAUGHING COW

She comes from the very best
laughing stock, raised high
in the Alps, on edelweiss.
Nothing can touch
her milk-white skin,
its lush lit-from-within quality.
Sauntering up the sweet-grass slopes,
the little lead clanger in the throat
of her bell punctuates every guffaw
rising from her satiny maw.

Humor can be a hard cud to chaw
but she does it, time and again:
works a mouthful of woe
through the hungry twists
of her recesses. The result:
purest squirts of creamy mirth, waxy wheels
of cackling cheese, sticks of salt-free butter
dropped like bad puns into a waiting pail.
It's side-splitting work, this effusion of milk,
but the comic cow's not one to shirk.

La vache qui rit
they call her, and have even named a cheese
after her. Favored snack of the major
airlines, her gleeful countenance
looks up from a foil-wrapped triangle
balanced on a stack of water
wafers, beaming with wit and good
will. Oh sacred, jolly cow,
every time I eat of your levity
I fly.

D o w n

By the river's edge,
beside a bridge,
a troop of wild geese
live.

All day they bear
the white heat of my secret
heart.

Is it a sin if I desire
a gosling the color
of dandelion?

Each time, what I want
is to break bread
in silent communion,
but they rush up,
flapping and honking.

Once, near dusk,
I watched the troop
amble, double-file,
toward bed.

Their eyes burned
with holy purpose; they moved
with so

deliberate a step
it seemed hypnosis fueled
their passage.

Will you believe me
if I tell you geese
glow in the dark?
They drop their down
in the high grass.

One Hundred Days of a Hermit Crab

Week 1

Picked up, you crumple,
tuck, napkin-style,
into the throat

of the shell, the tip
of your biggest claw
unable to withdraw

from the lonesome brink of light.
Beyond, a conch-like face
of galactic size–pink-white,

with an opening like a black hole–
waits to draw you in, swallow.
How long does it take to feel safe?

In a moment your antennae straighten
and make of themselves divining rods,
tap feebly the nearest air, pause,

then plunge
you back into the dazzling
whorl again.

Week 5

At night, you dream of your youth.
Breezes slick
with salt and spoiled coconut milk

shiver across your right pincer.
Twenty feet above ground,
tucked into the crown

of a palm,
you obey the soulful call
of the moon

to climb down, enter
the silver foam. Slap!
and souuggghh go the waves. Slap!

you pluck a morsel,
still dripping,
from the foam. All

around you, hundreds of crabs
lift morsels to mouths
with delicate claws,

bobbing and swirling,
busily eating,
even as a man

standing at the water's edge
casts his net and skims
you still dripping from the foam.

Week 8

Preternaturally ponderous,
lazy because encumbered, *Coenobita clypeatus*,
my land hermit crab?

Hardly. Your shell
less helmet
than headdress, not

a ballerina
but a chorus line,
you cannot walk but you conga,

the bright batik
of your turban
shell gently bobbing

above the Folies Bergere
of your promenading;
all by yourself, a caravan crossing

the wind-whitened sand
of your cage.
Other days you emerge

from your shell
Philippe Petit
to conquer the driftwood's Olympic height:

unabashed,
displaying your skill,
and grateful for the chance.

Week 12

Well, anyone could have made
the same mistake!
Not having read the appropriate page

in the *Hermit Crab: Pet
Owner's Manual*, yet,
I couldn't imagine

what ailed you, crab,
burrowing in the sand,
no more my Charlie Chaplin

but a weak Houdini
disappearing.
Next morning, when you were clearly

dead, I peered
for the last time into
the beautiful funnel—

your shell-cum-casket.
Your big claw, once smooth,
mottled coral and russet,

was withered.
Tearfully, I touched it
and *JEHOSAPHAT!*

it clung to my hand,
flaked off, then drifted down
to the floor: molted.

And there you were, deep
in your mortal coil, asleep,
not dead, newly-minted

and pink as a baby's
bottom, soft-shell
inside your rock-hard outer shell.

Week 15

Now when I pick you
up, you blast forth
from your shell, a blue

note wrung
from Triton's horn,
the storm

of your own teacup.
Face to face, you rap
at my lower lip

to gain entrance to the cave.
Open, Sesame ! you rap,
stalk eyes tilted up

at mine, until I laugh,
and still you tap
the gleaming-white

stalactite and stalagmite,
listening to the echo whistling
in my mouth when I say your name.

THE PURPLE THANKSGIVING TURKEY

The day after Thanksgiving
I discover him
penned in a front yard along
the main street in town,

the sight enough to cause
accidents, really: orchid-purple
from crown to claw, his
magnificent wattle wild magenta

against the pale-ale haze of November.
The great bird struts,
tersely placing his old man's feet
here and there on his square

of lawn, splaying his cock-sure dignity
to the shocked grins and hornblasts
from passing cars. No one guesses, yet,
that a turkey dyed purple

will soon die purple: death by dye,
dyed death. Least of all the turkey.
He feels reborn; thinks life is a mat
of green underfoot with kernels

and grain smashed into it,
a criss-cross gleam of metal
netting the sky.
I am just one of the many

who have followed the stars home
to see him. He knows this,
nods delicately

when I kneel, bearing gifts.

WITH THE FLESH REMAINING

Whitehorse, Yukon Territory...a horse found this fall near the Alaska border...is one of the best-preserved Ice Age animals discovered in North America. The dark chestnut hide is complete with blond mane and tail. Also recovered were a right foreleg with the flesh remaining, a couple of bones and stomach contents. Archaeologist Ruth Gotthardt said ...the carcass was so well-preserved that it still smelled strongly of dead horse..

—Boston Globe, December 25, 1993

The archaeologist is elated.
Out of the creek where it drank
its last, out of the overhanging bank
that collapsed in one fell shrug of earth,
grass, broken flowers, worms,
the ghost of Whitehorse returns.

That he was beautiful surprises
no one. Twenty-six thousand years
ago he lowered his tow-head,
poised a hoof against the tide's
insistent rub. Now his bones rest
in a velvet box every bit as black

as the silt that preserved
them. Though his hide,
his tail, even his last meal,
were rescued from the soil,
what could not be conveyed
from the ancient bed was what

Whitehorse kept—over millennia
of frost, gales, Northern Lights—
to himself. Whitehorse steps back into
time wrapped in his inimitable death,
his presence in this newer landscape
as lingering, as singular,

as it was in life.

WHEN YOU LOVE SOMEBODY

It was a very hot day in June when we first saw Lula...an eighteen month old pig-tailed macaque monkey. She had been in England for one year, now she was for sale...We will never sleep if we don't try to help her (I said, so we) went straight back to get her.

—Stan and Beryl Harrison, Derbyshire Times, January 1993

Like most babies, she was helpless,
too small to send back
where she belonged, where, without
a mother's protection, she wouldn't live.

Nothing at all like Singapore,
but Beryl and Stan did their best,
built their foundling pig-tailed macaque
a good-sized cage

in a garden in the heart
of England. "More like a child,"
they had to admit; though Lula was
"happy" she was also "destructive,"

frequently capable
of biting the hand
that watered, fed, scooped, caressed,
locked the cage door

before it left. During a snowstorm
twenty years on, after
the heat in her cage conked
out, Lula was brought

before the fireplace
in the family home.
She lived inside from that day on,
dressed in clothes a much-loved

daughter might have worn.
The nappy she sometimes wore
was just a precaution—
no point in learning

self-control
this late in life—
and the pram Stan
wheeled her around in,

that, too, was necessary,
for lugging Lula was like
shouldering a tombstone!
"Difficulties and sacrifices,"

that's what it cost
to keep Lula at home,
but Beryl and Stan
"loved her to bits

and didn't care."
What else could they do
but shut their ears
to those who claimed

that their kind of care-
taking was unfit
for beast, that the habit
they'd fallen into—Lula

sleeping at the foot
of the bed—wasn't helping her be
what she was: a macaque.
She grew plump, then fat, her fur

thick and shiny from the daily
brush, her great eyes glowing
with the entrancing routine
of being served, dressed,

carted, kissed.
Did she lose the muscular grace
that jungle life cultivates, did
her wiles fade, did she miss

sex? There's no telling
how she might have lived
under different circumstances,
how harried or how rest-

ful her days. Some declared Lula's
pampering cruel. "Nonsense.
When you love somebody
you know what's best for them."

LESSONS OF THE EYE TEETH

LESSONS OF THE EYE TEETH

Every smile hides a bite,
the fear of being left out;

in the cheek of every scowl
is a wad of hope.

The need for caution is real:

the saber-toothed tiger could be killed by a kiss,
the history of the world is engraved in the tusks of elephants.

If only the mouth could see itself,
could taste the danger in every hunger.

Nothing tastes as good as it looks,
but the eye teeth, just learning to see,
can't discern this.

Inside the blind, soft cave
of the mouth, Wisdom arrives
in a burst of pain, and too late.

A Watched Pot
Never Boils

Use a lid. Walk away.
A clove can be crushed while you wait.

When the china begins to hum,
dusty and fragile, listen closely:

every vibration it ever heard
repeats inside its mineral heart.

There is a stopped bottle sitting in the chilly dark
that must be shaken.

There is a hard lump of pleasure
that comes with its own knife.

When at last a cloud of steam
forms above the pot, something hard

can soften, something dry moisten, something raw
become the source of life.

Prepare to dip fingers into strange plates,
exchange glances with the host.

Prepare to sleep with the cut juice of garlic
informing every other smell the night creates.

By daylight, the pot hangs on the wall,
taunting the kettle until it weeps,

the remains of last night's feast
derange the tablecloth. Whatever else

it covers up, the fabric cannot hide
its checkered past.

EVERY KNOT WAS ONCE STRAIGHT ROPE

The return address said Death Row,
State Prison, Starke, Florida,
the same prison holding Ted Bundy
safe from random revenge. The correspondent
had the job of death house orderly,
which is to say: would live. After
a few wrong turns and twists,
he now grasped the absolute necessity
of keeping all one's ducks in a row
(as with pins in a bowling alley,
the impulse is the same: make a straight
line out of a sprawl, then mow
it down.) Anyway, he'd gotten your name
from a pen pal magazine
and wanted you to know
about the life on Death Row.
Ted Bundy was a "fine man," full
of interesting tales, and he himself,
given the chance, could unravel
all mystery about that man, any man.
Envisioning the orderly at your door
one night, a tangle of homicidal pals in tow,
you declined to discover how,
out of the plowed row of a condemned life, hope
springs up like a new-sown crop,
even as the knot woven into the noose
was once, make no mistake, straight rope.

IT'S NOT OVER UNTIL
THE FAT LADY SINGS

First you're struck by the violins:
That marsh full of reeds, sawing.

Next, you succumb to the woodwinds:
Grouse in the grass, the slow step of the cat.

All at once, a cymbal crash.
The great oak splits and a curtain drops.

Quiet your hands: it is only an act,
One scene in a life that looms Titanic,

Ramming against something so much
Larger than itself, the tip is all you see

As you start to sink. Now the one who
Embodies meaning steps from the wings.

She tells it like it is, she brings the house down.
And plenty more where that came from.

No Use Crying over Spilt Milk

Get ahead of the game: seek spills out.
Accidents wait in every room of the house.

Stanch the flow as best you can.
This is blood that doesn't clot.

Now it's a lake, serene as skin.
Now it's a blanket, spread for sin.

Too much of a good thing
Can't be contained.

My cup runneth over.

What's lost is lost.

BETWEEN TWO STOOLS YOU FALL TO THE GROUND

Between two stools is a treacherous gulf.
I thought you knew better than to fall
Victim to the tiger-traps the self
Sets in its bid to fail. Between two stools is a gulf
Wide as death, real as dreams. The stealth
With which fear trails our every wish! All
We had fell apart between two stools, that gulf
I heard in your voice, and into which I am falling.

MISERY LOVES COMPANY

Come in, sit down.

No one's a stranger here,
no one a disappointment.
Let us read together

the story of the man
in the garden at Gethsemane,
who, contemplating a death

worse than his fate,
insisted his companions stay
close while he prayed.

Though he pretended anger
when they fell asleep,
he in fact found their

disloyalty a relief,
a smooth excuse to feel
something other than grief.

Maybe you have found yourself
afraid of the dark
and full-grown?

Come then, sit.
My rooms have never been larger.
I have added a side door

and jettisoned
every extraneous
piece of furniture.

I feel as gregarious
as that man in the garden,
who nonetheless

came to see
by the light of a blood-red dawn,
in every companion, some form of betrayal.

IF WISHES WERE HORSES

Toss a penny, hide
a tooth, close
your eyes and blow
the candles out.

Unsure of the full
urge of your desire?
Scratch ears, proffer fruit.
Then dig in spurs.

It feels like peril,
like falling in a dream.
Your night mare rears
and gallops from the barn.

Do your hands
clutch the reins?
Let go, grip the mane.
Do words leave

your throat in a scream?
Take the bit
between your teeth,
get the word

from the horse's
mouth. She's a nag: flog
her. She's white: ride
her like a breaking wave.

She's dark: she has all
your secrets by heart.
She will break your neck
on the finish line.

WHEN HELL FREEZES OVER

When hell freezes over we can walk on it,
clear to the other side.

For once, the waves are still,
the air free of smoke.

Wind from the North brings snow
and the sudden flowers of frost.

We have no idea of future,
no hunger for the past.

At last we can see ourselves
inside the frozen glass.

Here, the eyes lined with forgiveness.
Here, the heart cracked open with love.

Here, the dreams we did not have.
Here, faith. Here, the second chance.

Too soon, the bonfire's built.
Flames lap heaven's gate.

Arm-in-arm we skate,
over the breaking ice.

You Can Lead a Horse to Water

Way down the field, where the ground
was humped as the back of a dragon
and none of us ever went,

the horses stopped grazing and lifted
their heads. It was a Maine
summer, the midday heat

coming upon us like a sneeze,
a violent, brief strength
under which the horses ranged,

gliding over the green in a knot
of bronze. I'd grow drowsy
watching them

drift like bees,
silent, intent, woven
into the landscape

in a way
I thought I could never be, my
absurd awareness of *self*

the hole in the whole.
I remember the alien peace I felt,
once, when I tried to embrace

the colt, his swollen barrel
of a stomach too huge to get
my arm around, but even so we communed

that way for a few
seconds, and, for those few seconds,
I belonged to the scene, I was unbroken.

At the end of the day,
when I fed them meal and hay
from the barn, there was a protocol

the horses followed:
to each his own
dish, and all ate

with abandon, staring blindly
as they champed. Later, they might
move toward the trough

at the side of the barn,
but I rarely saw them drink
from it, as though drinking were a private devotion

not to be witnessed.
When I think of that trough,
I think of the day

I found a kitten
sealed like a fly in amber
in its depth. The barn cats

had hardly looked pregnant,
and then there were two kittens,
and then there were two deaths,

the first one
kicked, and the second
drowned. Seamlessly found,

seamlessly lost. The barn cats
frisked the back field, unfazed.
I buried the kitten with a stiff

efficiency. Night sank.
The horses bowed their heads
to drink.

Any Port in a Storm

Once it was a parrot that caught my eye,
black hairs on a dark arm;
in the teeming markets of those seaside

towns, the quiet remove of the natives.
I made it my business to assimilate,
to embrace each port as though it were haven.

Now I'm blown to your shore, strange as any other.
I look to the treetops where the monkeys gossip
and think someday I'll stand underneath

and gather fruit, rich round skulls I'll crack
for their milk. I think we'll go all the way back
to innocence, when every part of a flower

is a surprise, shelter our sex in a weave of sticks
like a pair of bower birds, petals and shells
from the forest arranged on a mat of moss

the color of emeralds. That's what I want—
some ritual of display, fanfare for the foreigner.
Instead of storms and doldrums,

give me chameleons underfoot, dark
green shade the very thirsty can drink.
How I got here I cannot say.

There's Safety in Numbers

One is a cradle
high in a tree top.

One is a candle.

One is a match.

Never fear one, for one is the raft,
the journey across water,
the island, the new start.

To be one, you must stand
apart, see the hands
that reach to hold,
see the knife.

One has the singular comfort
of sight.

Two is a tug of war.

Or, two is a lifeline,
a ladder.

Two provides each half
a mirror.

With two, the whole
hangs in the balance.

When one falls,
the other carries.

Three is the Hen who made bread
while the rest of the farmyard
laughed.

Three is the Little Engine that could.

Three is the family,
a pyramid.

Three juggles,
gives piggybacks,
links arms, sallies forth.

Three is a force to be reckoned with.

Four is a place
to hide, a steep-roofed
mountain cabin,
fire within.

Climb four
to the sacred burial ground,
outpost and guard's
tower.

Nothing escapes four's notice,
for four sees the forecast,
the trees
and the forest.

Five is the opening
of a cave.
Five is a fish hook,
an arm crooked
to scoop something up.

Five is when the body,
curled in dreams,
forms a sea horse,
a snake. Five can be
a belief system:

the optimism of a starfish,
whose torn limbs
regenerate.
At five, candles in a cake
light themselves.

Six has a secret cache of jewels.
Six is pregnant and overdue.
Six stoops to woo, talks to
Strangers, breaks the rules.
Six plays to win and wins,
Nobody's fool. With

Six you get egg roll, not egg
On your face. Six is a
Siren with a serpent's grace.
Six is a perfect number, it seems:
She cycles, she surrenders,
She divides, she reigns.

Seven is a desert
to be crossed,
a weedy stretch
of bad luck,
the short end
of a wishbone
pulled apart.

Everywhere you see
despair, Seven has been
and gone, a moving
plague, a curse
in action. Swim
the Seven Seas
and die young.

Then take up Seven's
staff and walk.
Scan the black above
for the Seven
visible planets,
the Seven glittering
rooms of heaven.

Now point Seven's
divining rod toward
the world and its
wonders. Imagine
creating all this by
yourself. Do so.
You've got one week.

Eight hates
To repeat itself
But can't help
Doing so.
Eight hears its
Own Echo,
The self's inner
Affirmation.

Ergo, Eight's
Ego is round,
Unbound by
Fear of failure.
Eight is the
Heart's ideal,
The face
In the water.

Nine is a harm-
ful habit. To see how
the nine rivers of Hell
become the same waterfall,
rocky pool below,
repeat this charm:
nine lives out
of nine, I'd choose
the same.

Ten is a whisper beneath the willow by the waterfall.
Ten is a pillar in the great town hall.
Ten is a pitchfork beside a hay bale.
Ten is a lover scaling the wall.
Ten's trail skirts an oval lake.
Ten is a narrow escape.
Ten is a mistake.
Ten's heart breaks,
Dreaming of
One.

Dedications

"Believe It Or Not" is for Bill Kimball

"Chain Poem" is for Ruth Hall

"Every Knot Was Once Straight Rope" is for Barry Duncan

"With The Flesh Remaining" is for Mark Anderson

"Gretel, Lost" is for John Mahoney

"Memento Mori" is for Helen Walker

Cover: the mythical human race known as Blemmyes.

"And in another isle toward the south dwell folk of foul stature and of cursed kind that have no heads. And their eyes be in their shoulders."

The Travels of Sir John Mandeville, circa 1366

Thanks to the Spencer Collection, The New York Public Library, Astor, Lenox and Tilden Foundations, for the use of the blemmye image.